ABBY WAMBACH

BY RYAN NAGELHOUT

Gareth Stevens
PUBLISHING

Please visit our website, www.garethstevens.com. For a free color catalog of all our high-quality books, call toll free 1-800-542-2595 or fax 1-877-542-2596.

Library of Congress Cataloging-in-Publication Data

Names: Nagelhout, Ryan, author.
Title: Abby Wambach / Ryan Nagelhout.
Description: New York : Gareth Stevens Publishing, [2017] | Series: Sports
  MVPs | Includes index.
Identifiers: LCCN 2015046721 | ISBN 9781482446470 (paperback) | ISBN
  9781482446395 (library bound) | ISBN 9781482446296 (6 pack)
Subjects: LCSH: Wambach, Abby, 1980—Juvenile literature. | Women soccer
  players–United States–Biography–Juvenile literature. | Soccer
  players–United States–Biography–Juvenile literature.
Classification: LCC GV942.7.W36 N34 2017 | DDC 796.334092–dc23
LC record available at http://lccn.loc.gov/2015046721

Published in 2017 by
Gareth Stevens Publishing
111 East 14th Street, Suite 349
New York, NY 10003

Copyright © 2017 Gareth Stevens Publishing

Designer: Samantha DeMartin
Editor: Ryan Nagelhout

Photo credits: Cover, pp. 1, 13 Mike Zarrilli/Getty Images Sport/Getty Images;
p. 5 Dennis Grombkowski/Getty Images Sport/Getty Images; p. 7 Brian Bahr/Getty
Images Sport/Getty Images; p. 9 Christian Peterson/Getty Images Sport/Getty
Images; p. 11 Brian Blanco/Getty Images Sport/Getty Images; p. 15 The Washington
Post/The Washington Post/Getty Images; p. 17 Stuart Franklin - FIFA/Getty Images;
p. 19 Debby Wong/Shutterstock.com; p. 21 (Abby) Christof Koepsel/Getty Images
Sport/Getty Images; p. 21 (trophies) Incomible/Shutterstock.com.

Printed in the United States of America

CPSIA compliance information: Batch #CS16GS: For further information contact Gareth Stevens, New York, New York at 1-800-542-2595.

CONTENTS

Boldface words appear in the glossary.

American Hero

Abby Wambach is the greatest American women's soccer player of all time. She was born June 2, 1980, in Rochester, New York. Wambach holds many **international** records. She's also a Women's World Cup **champion** and two-time Olympic gold medalist.

Growing Up

Mary Abigail Wambach was the youngest of seven children. She played soccer and basketball like her sisters. When she was 5, she scored 27 goals in her first three soccer games. Wambach often played on boys' soccer teams growing up!

Wambach and her mom

7

High School Striker

Wambach played high school soccer in Rochester, New York. She played forward, or striker. When she was a senior, her team lost the state title, or championship, game. They were up 3-0, but lost in double **overtime**.

9

Gator Great

In 1998, Wambach went to **college** at the University of Florida. She played four seasons for the Gators. She set school records in goals, assists, game-winning goals, points, and **hat tricks**. She was All-Southeastern **Conference** four times and won conference Player of the Year twice.

For Her Country

Wambach started playing for the United States in 2001. She won gold at the 2004 Olympic Games. In the 2007 Women's World Cup, she scored six goals in six matches. She missed the 2008 Olympics because of a broken leg.

Going Pro

After college, the Washington Freedom of the Women's United Soccer Association (WUSA) **drafted** Wambach. She won the WUSA title there in 2003. She has also played and coached for the MagicJack in the Women's Professional Soccer (WPS) league.

Seeking Gold

The United States finished second in the 2011 Women's World Cup. They lost to Japan in a shootout. The next year, Wambach led the United States to a gold medal in the London Olympics. She scored five goals in six matches.

Setting Records

In 2013, Wambach broke Mia Hamm's record for career international goals. She also married Sarah Huffman. They played together on the Western New York Flash in the National Women's Soccer League (NWSL).

World Cup Glory

Abby played in her fourth World Cup at age 35 in 2015. The United States beat Japan, 5-2, to win their fourth World Cup. Wambach finally won the title after four World Cup **tournaments**. Later that year, Wambach announced she was **retiring** from soccer!

TROPHY CASE

US Soccer Female Athlete of the Year

2003 2004 2007
2010 2011 2013

Olympic Gold Medal

2004 2012

FIFA Women's World Player of the Year 2012

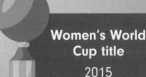

Women's World Cup title

2015

GLOSSARY

champion: a person or team that is the overall winner of a contest or sport

college: a school attended after high school

conference: a group of athletic teams

draft: to pick players for a team. Also, the act of picking players for a team.

hat trick: scoring three goals in a game

international: involving two or more countries

overtime: an extra period of time needed to find a game's winner

retire: to stop doing a job because of age or ability

tournament: a contest of skill played by many different teams

FOR MORE INFORMATION

BOOKS

Bankston, John. *Abby Wambach*. Hockessin, DE: Mitchell Lane Publishers, 2014.

McDougall, Chrös. *The Best Soccer Players of All Time*. Minneapolis, MN: ABDO Publishing, 2015.

Porter, Esther. *Abby Wambach*. North Mankato, MN: Capstone Press, 2016.

WEBSITES

Abby Wambach
biography.com/people/abby-wambach-21331043
Find out more about Wambach's life on this Biography.com page.

Abby Wambach
ussoccer.com/players/2014/03/15/05/05/abby-wambach
Learn more about Wambach's career and family on this US Soccer site.

INDEX